For those on a journey to self-love,

When the world tells you not to love.

*Coffee, a Notebook and Self Love*

## Suraj

The Sun

## Dhuan

Smoke

## Pahara

Mountains

## Chand

The Moon

*Coffee, a Notebook and Self Love*

**Suraj**

The Sun

.

You look at me,

I get weak in the knees,

You tell me you love me,

My clothes fall,

Like the leaves,

On the trees.

***Autumn***

I love you,
Well at least I think I do.
I don't know,
Maybe I just like you.

Imagine if I told you,
That in each moment we speak,
My feelings grow,
I'm in deep.

I pluck up the courage,
Fear takes over me,
I want you on top,
All over me.

Each time I scroll,
I see your face,
I lose control
You're beautiful.


**I want you to know.**

I love you,
Well at least I think I do.
I don't know,
Maybe I just like you.

In a moment of madness,
I crave you,
In a moment of sadness,
I rely on you.

Everything is you,
The world revolves,
But it isn't the same,
Without you.

In a moment of honesty,
I tell you how much you mean to me,
You probably won't even believe me,
I'm scared you will leave me.


**I don't want you to know.**

Never have I heard,

A voice so sweet,

You call to say hello,

My heart skips,

A beat.

I think of you and I,

I get a shiver down my spine,

You are so beautiful,

I could only wish you were mine.

I dream of our sweet embraces,

My lips on your lips,

Our hearts racing,

So divine.

I don't want to keep this in,

You should know,

If we are together,

I promise,

It's win – win.

All this talk about love,

How can I be expected,

To put someone else,

Above,

My feelings for me.


- ***Self Love***

And when the time comes,

They won't utter,

Those three words,

You have longed for.


They will tell you,

With conviction,

Without apprehension,

<u>No matter what.</u>

-     *Unconditional*

As I gain another year of life,

All my thoughts surround yours,

The life you were never given,

The life you could have had.

I failed you,

I disappointed you,

I hope that you forgive me,

My sweet baby.

The love we shared,

Is a love that can never be replaced,

Forever in my heart,

You'll always be mine.


-    *To my unborn child.*

After night falls,

Thoughts of you consume me,

Who am I kidding,

Thoughts of you,

Always consume me.

Once upon a time,

You saved me,

From the darkness,

I can only hope,

I do the same for you.

I opened my soul,

And for the first time,

I realised that,

I wasn't alone.

We all have that one,

That person,

That without a shadow of a doubt,

Could knock on your door,

And you will still,

Welcome them in.


-   *Until the end of time.*

And sometimes you have to accept,

That they are not the one for you,

Even though,

You are the one for them.

\-      *Unrequited love.*

It wasn't until,

You showed me all your darkness,

That I exposed,

My light.

-    *True colours.*

When I see those eyes,

Its flight,

Or fight.

We were different,

Opponents.

You made the first move,

In return I made one too.

Along the way we pawned parts of ourselves,

In the hopes we would win.

Until we were in a position,

Where we were captured.

<u>Checkmate.</u>

I can only describe it as an invasion,

It was calm,

Until you bought,

The storm.

This has weighed on me,

For far too long,

I'll tell you,

I love you,

Then,

You'll say it too.

-Dreams.

I want you to want me.

Not to need me.

Need tells me you don't have a choice.

Want means you do,

And I want you to choose me.

What could I do?

Just as the sun rises without fail,

Was the same way I fell for you.

-    *Inevitable*

Each of us is like the universe,

There is no centre.

Just countless,

Bits,

And pieces,

That somehow,

Found themselves,
**Together.**

Now take my hand,

We may never have a chance,

Forget your inhibitions,

Can we have this dance?

\-    *Chivalry isn't dead.*

For a moment,

I close my eyes,

Take a deep breath,

Then believe.


That if Aladdin could be with Jasmine,

It could be you with me.


If Cinderella got Prince Charming,

Then maybe we're meant to be.


I believe in fairy tales,

One day,

It will be the story of you and me.

You're my worst enemy,

But also my best friend.

It will be us,

Until the end.

You inspire me,

More than I thought,

Someone could.

I want to try express,

All these things,

Going around in my head.

I'll paint all my feelings,

Write my thoughts,

You are the source.

-    *Muse.*

Though you may not be here,

I want to fulfil your biggest fears.

Visit the places you loved,

And the places you'd never been.

Read your favourite books,

Then read them again.

Finish all the things on your bucket list,

Try to do the things I know you wished for.

Tell my children all about you,

Recite stories about all you'd been through…

…Though you may not be here,

You will always be here,

Forever present,

Forever near.

Your sweet words,

Replay in my head,

For some reason,

I still can't believe,

All those beautiful things,

You said.

It's amusing to me,

When someone mentions,

Your name,

I smile without hesitation,

It's no longer a game.

I don't just write for me,

I do it for,

The lost souls,

The misunderstood,

The lovers,

The fighters,

The ones who wish they could,

The heart broken,

The heart breakers,

The ones who wake up wishing they didn't,

The ones who didn't wake up and wish they did,

For the strong one,

I write for everyone,

That even includes you.

I lost sleep over you last night,

I don't think I could bare,

That I'd hurt you,

Made you feel despair.

I try to keep you at arm's length,

Because I'm scared,

That when I see you,

I'll see sense.

I was so content,

Then you walked,

Straight in,

I wasn't ready,

For this to begin.

I couldn't help it,

Believe me,

I tried to,

But there you were,

Making me weak,

The sweetest kind of,

Sin.

I remember the universe,

When I didn't know,

You were in it,

I'd never go back,

Not even for a **minute.**

With you,

The bad days don't seem so bad,

I look at the world in a whole new light,

It's just like you,

So beautiful,

So bright.



With you,

The world doesn't seem so cold,

You took this little heart of mine,

Put it in drive,

Even made me want to put in overtime.

I want to be the best version of me,

But you make me want to be,

Even better.

I don't want a love like everyone else's.

You have the weight of the world on your shoulders,

Yet you look weightless.

You ask if I miss you,

As you look deep in my eyes,

My throat gets dry,

Mind goes numb,

The cat's got it,

It's taken my fucking,

Tongue.

I couldn't talk to you,

So I wrote to you,

Told you things,

I want you to know,

Then I locked it away,

To save it for,

The day.

-     *If that day ever comes.*

I sip my coffee,

It's funny how similar,

It tastes compared to you,

Bittersweet.

If they are on your mind constantly,

That is your heart shouting,

Listen to me.

You keep running, when I don't want you to.

-    **J**

Enjoy your own company,

Because ultimately,

You are the one,

You sleep in bed with every night,

The one you bathe with,

Eat your food with,

Every single day,

If you cannot enjoy you,

How will you ever truly,

Be happy with you.

I see something in you,

I don't know what to do,

It caught my eye,

Like the sunset on a summers evening,

It mesmerised me,

Like the moon on a winters night.

I could write sonnets and make them all about you.

Make it clear just how much I feel as if I want you.

Not knowing if you really want me too.

I see so many of my traits in you that it scares me, because I know that you feel as confused as I do. That you spend hours of your day wondering about me, even if we're not talking.

That you lie awake at night thinking of all the things you would do if you were next to me.

I know you feel it too.

I know you're not ready,

I don't think I am too,

All I can say,

Is that,

I don't want life,

Without you.

Maybe,

This was meant to be,

I guess,

We'll just wait,

And see.

We both know,

It's only going to end,

One of two ways,

But either way,

I'm going to fall,

And I think,

You want me to.

I don't know how you function on such little sleep,
How you force yourself out of bed to take on the week.

I don't know how you keep your light so bright,
How you smile yet you struggle night after night.

I don't know how you have the courage to keep going on,
How you cope with days so long.

I didn't know strength until I saw you,
Just like everyone else,
I am in awe too.

One day,

You'll feel like they don't deserve you,

The next,

You'll feel like you don't deserve them.

- *Trials and tribulations.*

My heart says, just go with it.

My mind says, don't be so naïve.

My body says, I miss you.

My soul says, I love you.

Maybe this time,

It's for keeps.

- *Searching for a pot of gold.*

I don't know what it is,

There are certain people,

You'll meet in life,

Where there is this,

Instant connection,

Affection,

It doesn't matter,

How much time goes by,

That when you lock eyes,

It's like time,

Stands still.

I lie awake so many nights,

My mind wanders,

Through all the planets,

Galaxies,

The universe,

And still,

It always starts,

And ends,

With you.

A touch of uncertainty,

Mixed with,

An air of fear,

I'm waiting,

Silently,

For you,

My dear.

I spent all this time,

Learning to self-love,

Put my relationship with me,

As a top priority.

Then here you come,

And knock me off the top spot,

But what can I do,

Trust my relationship with me,

Or my relationship with you.

I remember your lips,

So vividly,

I close my eyes,

I can feel them,

So soft,

Was it even real?

You are just like the excitement,

When I see those lemons.

You are just like the anticipation,

As I cut into them.

You are just like the thrill,

As I grind the salt.

You are mouth-watering.

*Salty Lemons*

**Pahara**

Mountains

**Even in the midst of chaos,**

**Remember who you are.**

**I wrote this for you,**

You,

Who used to call me on those late nights,

Thinking that you could hit it right,

But suddenly you'd be out of sight.


It's for you,

Who I bared it all too,

Gave you everything till you stepped,

Like I was shit on your shoe.


You who thought I'd wait till you were ready,

Selling dreams about us being steady,

When really,

We both knew you were already on to the next...

...It's for you,

Who claimed you could handle me,

It's funny coz you couldn't even get a handle on you,

Let alone me.


You,

Who was out here chanting catch flights not feelings,

Full of confidence,

Until you were left feigning for me.


*This is from me, without you.*

I won't block you,

It's a reminder of that luscious thing you used to taste,

A taste you cannot replace.

Not with another,

Because it will never be the same.

Sorry not sorry,

Because,

If you're reading this,

Wondering if this is about you,

It is.

You are too late.

It's your mind that plays the tricks,

It is foolish.

Imagine being so liberated,

You took a chance.

On a journey,

To make peace with my demons,

Each step,

Is one closer to freedom.

You pop back up,

Out of the blue.

You say,

You miss me.

Then ask,

If I miss you too.

I think you forgot,

All the things you did.

Maybe you remember,

And can't live with it.

I can't quite figure out,

What it is you want from me.

Remember baby,

It's no longer we…

...

You came out of the blue,

Now back into it you run.

Because you couldn't bear,

To be blinded by the sun.

It's not what you want to hear,

I know you don't want to know,

But best believe, tonight you're going to listen,

Even though you won't enjoy the show.

I need to get this off my chest,

Before I make my way onto the next,

Let you know what's deep within,

Like I'm about to confess my biggest sin.

I thought about you often,

At times I felt I needed you more than oxygen,

I wanted you to know me so bad,

In so deep, like I was going mad.

So mesmerising,

I couldn't help myself,

To be honest,

I wanted you all to my fucking self.

*I could have loved you,*
*I would have loved you,*
*I shouldn't love you.*

The day I'm over you,
Is the day I can look you in your eyes,
And tell you,
This is not what I want anymore.

The day I am over you,
Is the day I can bump into you,
And not feel an ounce of guilt,
About everything that happened.

The day I'm over you,
Is the day our long painfully beautiful history,
Is just that.

*History.*

I am the beach,
You are the sea,
You always come back,
When you miss me.

It will never be better,
It doesn't matter where you go,
The grass isn't going to be greener,
It doesn't matter where it grows.

**Irreplaceable.**

You try to pull me back,
I keep trying to move on,
What do you want?
You already won.

When you're around,
You make my heart race,
Not in a good way,
I'm tired of the chase.

I'm sorry if my work triggers you.
It's just that,
It comes to a point,
Where you have to,
Be true.

All the trauma you've had,
It took a part of you,
That you'll never get back.
But aren't you tried,
Of being so sad?

It happened,
And you may not like it,
But you can survive this.
If you're reading this,
You already did.

\-       **<u>Survivor</u>**

It took a while for me to see,

That your opinion,

No longer,

Means anything to me.


You consoled me,

Low key,

Tried to control me,

High key,

Made me think,

There was only me.


It took a while for me to see,

That deep down,

You knew,

You weren't good enough for me.


*-Epiphany.*

You see,

These tables,

They always turn,

I'm sorry not sorry,

This time,

You have to learn.

I have to stop wanting you, more than I want myself.

-   *Priority.*

To all my fellow writers,
Know that,
There is no wrong,
Or right here.

Write what you feel,
It is uncertain,
That you may feel that way,
Ever again.

She wasn't naïve,

She wanted to believe.

If you had another chance, would you risk it?

They say that I haven't witnessed a war,

And that I haven't fought battles,

If what they say is true,

Then why do I have all these scars?

I don't know what I'm more afraid of,

You breaking my heart,

Or,

Me breaking yours.

I am female,

A woman,

A lady in these streets,

Yet,

I am still,

The baddest bitch,

You ever did see.

I am part of my mother,
So generous,
So kind.
I am part of my father,
So giving,
With a strong mind.


I am the good,
I am the bad,
I am the best parts,
And the worst parts,
Of everyone around me.


Take me as I am,
I'm just me.

You want them.

They want them.

When they want you.

You want them.

*Whatever you're feeling will change how you read this.*

*Just like life, it will always be subjective.*

You are timeless,

A work of art.

Billions of people,

Spread all over this earth,

There is only one of you,

In billions,

Don't ever question,

Your worth.

I can sum it up in three little words,
***I miss you…***

…But I miss me more.

I'm sure many of you,
Just like me,
When things get rough,
We retreat,
We need quiet.

If you don't,
Let me explain it like this,
It's like,
Needing a chocolate bar,
When you're on a diet.

Who will save the <u>hero</u>?

Hero;

*<u>noun</u>*

1.                    <u>1.</u>

<u>a person who is admired for their courage, outstanding achievements, or noble qualities.</u>

They may be brown,

But we are all colours too.

Just because,

They've got more melanin than you,

Doesn't make them any better or any less than you.

We are so quick to point the finger,

Blame it on race,

For once why don't we sit?

Listen,

Slow the pace.

You'll never understand what it's like to be,

Something you're not,

A different race, religion or gender,

It's a shame,

That everyone seems to have an agenda,

A need to place blame…

Maybe it's time we,

Open our minds,

Hearts,

And ears.

\-      ***Shanti***

Don't be so hard on yourself,

You're only human,

Remember,

Life never pans out,

The way we planned out.

We're all on a ride,

Not knowing what's coming,

Not knowing where we're going,

Yet,

Here you are,

Still riding.

Close your eyes,

Tell yourself you can do it,

And eventually,

You will.

Some say I'm secretive,

But it's not even that,

When you get to know me,

Along with it comes loyalty,

And sometimes,

People are just not ready.

-    *I want to save you from myself.*

I care too much,

Too soon,

About too many people,

I forget that,

Because I care,

It doesn't mean,

They do too,

That's the problem,

I care too much,

Too soon,

About too many people,

Especially you.

Don't carry the weight on your shoulders,

Express it,

Let go of it,

Then breathe,

You'll feel so much lighter,

So much brighter,

So much closer to being back,

To the you,

We all once knew.

If it harms your heart,

It's not right for you,

Yes people change,

But it doesn't matter,

How much you want it,

Unless they want it too.

Just enjoy the happiness,

Whilst you have it,

If it's gonna fuck up,

It will fuck up,

But at least,

There's a silver lining.

If you begin to question you,

Then trust me baby,

It's not the one for you.

And just like most things,

It will hurt at first,

But as time goes by,

The pain will subside,

Or maybe you'll just get used to it,

But either way,

The day will come,

Where you will know,

The choice you made,

Was the right one.

I won't shit on your name,

Because you caused me pain,

I may not like you,

But I damn sure love you,

So when your name,

Caresses my lips,

It will simply be,

Because I miss,

Us.

Self love is only overrated to those who are not ready to love themselves yet.

Their time will come.

*I've been seeing a lot of things on social media about how self love is an overrated trend. Maybe it is another trend but it's so much better than the 'no feelings' trend. Finally society is encouraging people to face themselves, their trauma and their mental health to better themselves.*

*If thats overrated, then I guess we're overrated.*

Sometimes I sit alone,

In any favourite coffee shop,

Surrounded by people,

Having the deepest conversations,

Some having first dates,

And I feel content,

That I can sit here,

With nobody,

Because,

Unlike most,

I don't need anybody.

You don't need someone who wants to fix you,

You want someone who understands you and helps you fix yourself.

In this generation,

There's a habit of,

Forgetting,

That sex,

Doesn't fix everything.

It's used,

As a pawn,

And a distraction,

Everything it was never supposed to be.

I'm so lucky,

I can listen to,

The voices in my head,

My heart,

Put a pen to paper,

Then write it all down,

I often wonder,

If I couldn't do that,

What would I do?

I think I stopped believing in love,

That I only deserved the lies,

These Fuckboys told me.

That if I didn't make my body available,

Then my mind would be less attractive.

*I submitted to the wrong kind of love.*

It's the trauma, it plays tricks on you.

Makes you think that you're only worth,

The bad things what have happened.

It wants to **define** you.

There's going to be a moment.

When you see their number,

As you scroll through your phone,

And feel nothing.

- *Block and Delete.*

I try to be enough,

But as long as,

I'm enough for me,

That's all that matters.

I lay here lonely,

On a Friday night,

Netflix and chilling,

Mind filling,

With thoughts of you…

Baby, I miss you,

I know you do too,

Every time I get a message,

I hope that it's you,

When it isn't,

I feel cold,

Blue

Take a second,
Close your eyes,
And just breathe.

Now read this.

**You are an immaculate version of you,**

**You triumph,**

**You make mistakes,**

**But,**

**There will only ever be one,**

**You,**

**Nobody can,**

**Should,**

**Or will,**

**Compare.**

**Dhuan**

Smoke

*Coffee, a Notebook and Self Love*

They hurt us,

And so we hurt another.

They yearn for us,

Yet we yearn for another.


We are happy,

But we may be happier with another.

We are secure,

Still we risk it all with another.


*Utopia.*

My heart is heavy,
There's a weight,
A burden,
I cannot be rid of.

So consuming,
It has taken over me.
I cannot recall,
Life before.

*Amnesia.*

You indulge in reckless behaviour,
You only live once.
You tolerate their immoral decisions,
Everything happens for a reason.

You warrant the universe to take control,
What goes around comes around.
You endorse the neglect,
Absence makes the heart grow fonder.

*Excuses.*

Isn't it funny how time goes on,

Life gets in the way,

The memories fade but,

The hurt wants to stay.

The scars they don't show,

Just because you have another,

Doesn't mean the other,

Disappeared.

Those things you feel,

You could never show,

You have to move on,

Or society says so.

You'll never forget,

Remember when you said you were done

But deep down you thought,

They could have been,

**The one.**

I told you I was special,

You didn't believe me,

Now that you're alone,

Maybe you will see,

That everything,

You needed,

Wanted,

Craved,

Was standing right there,

**In front of you.**

We act as if,

We have all the time in the world,

Just like an hourglass,

It will run out.


Remember,

To make the most,

Of what you have,

Whilst you have it.

Time waits for no one.

**Don't tell me,**

That you can't commit,

As if to say,

You didn't speak,

With those beautiful lips,

And devote yourself,

To all those lies,

That you told me.


**Don't tell me,**

That you love me,

Whilst you,

Look deep in my eyes,

Leave my side,

Then tell her,

That you love her,

Too.

On darker days,

I watch life go on,

I'm at a standstill,

I look around,

There is nobody,

They are all,

*Gone.*

I ponder death frequently,

I wonder how life will be,

When there is no longer you,

No longer me.

- *Speculation*

Loving you is simply not an option anymore,

It's just not for me.

You dealt,

There was everything to play for.

Dealers left,

It was time for my move.

I placed my bet,

You raised it.

It was all in,

I was all in.

Your bluff you see,

I called it.

You folded.

Just like I knew you would.

With everything on the table,

You walked away.

There I sat with my cards to my chest,

The full house you didn't want.

The game changed when I met you,

No longer did I want to play.

I thought you wanted the same.

It wasn't until you were gone,

That I realised no longer playing,

Left me,

**Played.**

He said the timing wasn't right,

That he wasn't ready,

But what he really meant,

Was that he wasn't ready for me,

He never will be.

If you want to walk away,

Make sure you keep it moving,

Don't look back,

Because what was once yours,

Will never be yours again.

And sometimes you get so caught up,

Thinking,

Feeling like you're the only one.

Then reality hits,

Like a ton of bricks,

You were just another one.

*-Options.*

You say I am evil,

That's funny because,

You must be evil too,

Take a look,

At all the things you did,

Those things,

I could never do.

I saw you,

Waited patiently for the butterflies,

Imagine my surprise when,

They never arrived.

There's the mess that life throws at you,

And,

There's the mess you make yourself.

You were the latter.

I shouldn't have to ask you,

To step up and do all the things you said you would do.

Better yet,

I won't put up with you empty promises,

Fuck that shit boo.

Go tell them to someone,

Who doesn't know you well enough,

To believe you.

**I'm through with you**.

As we say goodbye,

My eyes fill,

With tears of love.

My biggest fear for so long,

Was to lose him,

He became so precious,

I lost,

**ME**.

They don't even know it yet,

But watching you be happy,

Will fuck them up more,

Than whatever they did,

To you.

Those others,

They pass the time,

Something to do,

Whilst I get over,


You.

Days like this,

Remind me of what could have been,

I think of you,

And all I can do is imagine,

Like it's some kind of dream.

-    *Woe.*

I stare at my phone,

Wait for your reply,

The seconds turn to minutes,

Before I know it,

An hour has gone by,

Each time I look,

A little more hope dies,

The anxiety builds,

I sit,

I cry,

But,

Most of all,

I wonder why.

I try to love life,

But it's not always that simple,

Some nights I go to bed,

Fall asleep hoping I don't wake up,

Some nights I'm awake,

Hoping to fall asleep.

I hate when you're in your feelings,

Everything's so intense,

I can't lie I'm tired,

It's stress,

Lack of control,

Like a black hole,

Someone take my soul.

Sometimes fall back,

Then recognise who wants you,

And who is just using you.

There's only so much fighting you can do,

For someone that doesn't see something,

Worth fighting for in you.

If things naturally distance,

You can only keep reeling in the closeness,

So much,

Before you're exhausted,

Tired,

Ready to let it go.

In distance there is clarity,

Just like,

In ignorance there is bliss.

\-      *Pretence*

If you leave someone with the what if,

It will haunt you,

Like a bad smell,

Forever you'll wonder,

What if I'd have stayed,

Spoken to them one last time,

Would things be the same.

I sit and watch,

And wonder how,

If,

I was just another girl,

Who fell for you.

That's the thing about people,

They can sell you whatever,

No matter how unrealistic,

Dreams,

Happiness,

Love,

Loyalty,

Then walk away,

And sell it to someone new.

Sometimes I cry for you,

But I cry for me too,

It upsets me,

That I couldn't see through,

All those things you said.

The love is unconditional; your presence in my life is not.

Sometimes there is nothing you can do,

You love someone,

But you know what you deserve,

Is more than what they can give.

You think I want to leave,

Like I woke up one morning,

And decided it was over for me,

Every day my soul craves for yours,

When I can't have it,

My heart pours,

You didn't take me seriously,

Like I would just wait,

Till you decided I was enough,

Or that you were ready,

I wonder what it is,

Is it you,

Is it me,

Either way,

I won't be around to see.

# Chand

The Moon

You haven't seen the half,
Of what I'm going to do to you,
Once I get my hands all up on you.

I'll have you on some Drake shit,
You're the best I ever had,
Until I get you on some J.cole shit,
Wishing you could hit it in the morning.

You said you think you're ready for me,
But let me remind you again,
Once you get this,
You might never get it again.

So take this opportunity to live your life at its best,
Come take a swim in this ocean,
Make you feel as if you've been blessed.

I see you, staring at me like that,
We can both feel the tension.
I know you miss this,
All the attention.

It was something else,
The way that I'd crave you.
Fantasising,
Imagine, all the things we could do.

I clocked it,
The way you come by.
So that I can just about catch you,
In the corner of my eye.

I can't even lie,
You look so damn fine.
That I have to take a little moment,
To recuperate my mind.

You made it clear,
You only want me for my body.
But I don't blame you,
I would want me too if I was you.

I'm not being arrogant when I say that,
I can tell by the way you look at me.
Your bedroom eyes undressed me,
It took seconds.

You want to look me in my eyes
Whist your hand caresses my thighs
Before you fulfil your one wish
You dive in for a kiss.

You seem shocked,
We're you not prepared for me.
I taste like nothing you've ever tasted before,
Sweet,
It's almost addictive.

**Devilish**

I don't think he gets it,
So let me help him understand.
When I laid eyes on him,
He became in demand.

There's something about him,
My heart beats quick,
He has rich chocolate skin,
I can't wait to have a lick.

His smile catches my eye,
Especially his lips,
So luscious,
I fantasise about our first kiss.

He's sly as fuck,
I know he dresses that way on purpose,
Blacked out or grey shorts,
It all makes me nervous...

It's the worst,
Because his voice turns me on,
Every time he speaks,
My mind feels gone.

I can't help but want him,
It's almost sick,
Wishing every day,
I'll get to try out his...

That look in your eyes,
Gets me every time,
You're thinking about spreading my thighs,
Before you slide deep inside.

I don't want you to hold back,
Leave our inhibitions at the door,
Tonight is the night,
You and I are going to become so much more.

You're about to see my ass twerk,
Let me go in and put in that work,
It's so good,
I can't help but gush and squirt.

The sheets are soaked,
You hit me with those deep strokes,
You know I love being choked,
Almost feels like my back fucking broke.

I can't even lie,

I want you.

I've waited too long,

I need to feel you.

I know you wanted me to wait,

To crave,

To yearn,

For you but baby it's about time you came through.

I know it's not a race to the finish line,

But trust me I will make you finish,

More than one time.

Life's short so we shouldn't waste any more time,

The only thing that needs to happen is you gripping my waist for the

first time.

I have no shame anymore,

When I say I'll do whatever you like,

Believe me baby,

I'll do whatever you like.

-    *King*

It's that look you give me,

It draws me to you,

You see right through me,

You know what I wanna do.


I hear your voice,

It sends shivers down my spine,

I get goose bumps,

Every time.


I don't think you understand,

That every time I see you,

I feel that tingle,

I get wetter and wetter the more that we mingle…

…More time when I see you,

The nerves they take over,

I smile and nod,

I can't talk when we're sober.


I look at your hands,

Can you wrap them around my neck,

Make your grip get tighter,

Baby keep me in check.


Just imagine your lips,

On my lips,

My lips,

On the tip.

I don't know how else to put it…

*..Baby,*

*I want to get to know you.*

So lay here,

Let me take away all your regrets,

For this place,

Will never harbour stress.


\-      *Safety.*

I came into you,

You came into me,

Our bodies,

Joint together.


-       Lock and key

Out of all the guys,

Whose fingers,

Have graced my thighs,

Yours are the only ones,

That send,

Shivers down my spine.

A gaze is all it takes for you to tell me you feel the same.

**I promise.**
**You won't know what to do with yourself after spending the night**
**with me.**

I want to take all of you,

All day,

All night,

Every position,

No fights,

Just us,

Reaching heights,

Lights,

Or no lights.

Those clothes you wear,

I don't even care,

I undressed you,

At first stare.

I look at you,

You look back.

*- Trouble*

Your voice inspires me.

Your face releases desires in me.

Your touch ignites fires in me.

You

*In*

Me

I need to know my body,

Better than anyone else does,

I'll spend each day feigning,

Then spend each night releasing.

*-Love Yourself.*

Your smell lingers,

I breathe it in,

Close my eyes,

I can't wait,

To be with you,

Again.

\-   *Lonely Nights*

Don't lie and say you don't miss the way,

I'd take your soul,

Make you lose control,

Until you couldn't deny,

That with me you felt whole.

The sun shines,

Those lilies,

You bought me,

Bloom.

Just like the sun,

I open my flower,

When you are,

Around me.

You kiss my lips,

Then,

You kiss my *lips*.

I see those scars on your body,

The healed wounds,

I see those wounds inside you,

I hope I can help heal those too.

Let's compare,

Me,

To all the other women,

You've ran through,

We both know,

That their hips didn't curve,

The same way mine do.

Their lips didn't taste,

Half as good as mine do.

Their walls didn't clench,

As tightly as mine do.

Their throats didn't feel,

The same way mine does.

They didn't give you,

The same things I do,

They couldn't make you,

Want to bow down,

And give all of you,

Like I do.

-   *Queen*

I'd rather spend my night dressed down for you,

Than dressed up for everyone else.

Every night,

After that night,

My body never came,

The same,

As it did that night.


-       *One night only.*

I feel you next to me,
You look me in the eyes,
I have to take a deep breath,
Instantly wet between my thighs.

Your scent seduces me,
I cannot resist,
When you are near me,
It's pure bliss.

Let our minds intertwine,
Our bodies mingle,
So intense,
We can feel that tingle.

Tonight let me show you,
How a real woman does it,
Anything to please you,
Let's keep it one hundred.

*Coffee, a Notebook and Self Love*

Printed in Great Britain
by Amazon